# TREES OF EDEN

## LINDA SIGAMONY

eBook Edition ISBN: 978-0-578-95059-4
Print Edition ISBN: 978-0-578-95060-0

Cover design: Courtesy of Cynthia S
Cover image: Courtesy of Thelma J

Published in the United States of America

*Dedicated*
*to*
*my dear parents*

*"Of every tree of the garden thou mayest freely eat: But of the tree of the knowledge of good and evil, thou shalt not eat of it: for in the day that thou eatest thereof thou shalt surely die"* (Genesis 2:16,17)

# Contents

# Contents

# Preface

God created all things good and for a purpose. He made heaven for His throne and earth for His footstool (Isaiah 66:1). He made the sun and moon, beasts and birds, grass and herbs, and trees that have fruit with seed in it for food and formed man of the dust and made him a living soul; He planted a garden eastward in Eden, and there He put the man "to dress it and to keep it" (Genesis 2:15).

When God's purpose is unfulfilled, creation is out of synchrony with the Creator. All of creation obeys the ordinances of God to this day, except man. Adam and Eve ate of the one forbidden tree, so God banished them from the garden. Adam lost his purpose, his own heart now needing some tending.

Jesus fulfils Adam's lost purpose. He redeems and tends human hearts. He prepares the heart and sows the seed - the Word of God, and brings forth streams of living waters to flow and trees with seed-bearing fruit to grow. On the resurrection morn, Mary Magdalene, not recognizing the risen Lord Jesus, thought He was the gardener (John 20:15); in Christ, indeed we see a Gardener, Sower and Reaper. What the land experiences during cultivation, the heart does, when Christ is at work.

Taste of the *Trees of Eden* and see the goodness of *The Tree of Life* that stands in the middle. Then sow the good seed into the world, so the world may become the garden of the LORD!

Chicago, 2021                                        Linda Sigamony

# The Fall and The Rise!

*"...she took of the fruit thereof, and did eat..." (Genesis 3:6 King James Version)*

God made the first man Adam and placed him in the garden of Eden. He commanded Adam not to eat the fruit of the tree of the knowledge of good and evil. God was in the garden; where God is, that is Higher Ground.

## The Fall

### Sin

God formed the woman out of the man for a helper. The woman, seeing the pleasant appearance of the forbidden fruit, and knowing that it could make her wise, and being tempted, did eat giving some to Adam, and great was their fall! Therefore, Adam's race is a fallen race, fallen from God's presence. The trees of the garden of Eden stand witness to this.

God put Adam in the garden, "to dress it and to keep it" (Genesis 2:15) and blessed saying, "[b]e fruitful, and multiply" (Genesis 1:28). After the fall, Adam could no longer tend the garden, but he has multiplied and replenished the earth with good and evil.

### Law

Sin continued after the fall; the earth was so overgrown with wickedness that God destroyed all the world with everything in it in flood, except Noah and his family and two of every kind of living creature. The flood did not wash away sin or evil, for they soon sprouted out of the earth. No amount of washing with water can cleanse the human heart.

God made a covenant with a promise to Abraham: "And I will give unto thee, and to thy seed after thee...all the land of Canaan, for an everlasting possession and I will be their God" (Genesis 17:8). While the Israelites journeyed through the wilderness, and before they entered The Promised Land, God gave the law through Moses. Did the people stop committing unrighteous or evil deeds? The Israelites continued in sin, which led to their exile from God's Land.

**The Rise**

Repentance

Was God's law inadequate to bring humankind back to God? Certainly not. The law is good, but man is insufficient. St. Paul writes, "...for by the law is the knowledge of sin" (Romans 3:20). Israel had priests who performed animal sacrifices for their sins and prophets who would call them to repent and turn to God from their wicked ways. Jesus, begotten of the Father, came into this world to lift the fallen human race to Higher Ground so they may worship God there. Jesus gave Himself as the perfect sacrifice for the sins of the world; this sacrifice calls for repentance. Forgiveness and cleansing will follow repentance, not by water but by the Word. Jesus said to His disciples, "Now ye are clean through the word which I have spoken unto you" (John 15:3). Cleansed by the Word, man shall walk on the highway of holiness.

Faith

A heart forgiven and cleansed becomes God's dwelling place; the King and His Kingdom will be there. Jesus spoke about the Kingdom of heaven in parables to the crowds and explained them to His disciples when He was alone with them because those without faith, "seeing see not; and hearing they hear not, neither do they understand" (Matthew 13:13). How then shall they receive the Kingdom? Without faith, it will be impossible to understand and do what heaven requires of us. Heaven is for the sanctified and justified, "...justified by faith without the deeds of the law" (Romans 3:28). The "law of faith" (Romans 3:27) fulfils and satisfies the law of Moses. What is the law of faith? "Thou shalt love the Lord thy God with all thy heart, and with all thy soul, and with all thy mind...Thou shalt love thy neighbour as thyself" (Matthew 22:37-39). The law of Moses is not in vain; it becomes meaningful to faith, and faith will obey. By repentance made holy, and with faith ready to obey, man shall rise to Higher Ground!

*　*　*

# True Worship

*"...Let my son go, that he may serve me..." (Exodus 4:23)*

To the Samaritan woman, Jesus said, "true worshippers shall worship the Father in spirit and in truth: for the Father seeketh such to worship him. God is a Spirit: and they that worship him must worship him in spirit and in truth" (John 4:23,24).

**Liberated to worship**

True worship is possible only when the spirit is set free from bondage. Jacob also called Israel, and his descendants were under bondage in Egypt, a pagan nation. Moses, who was raised in the King's palace in Egypt, identifying himself with his people- the Hebrews, leaves the luxury of the court. God called Moses at the burning bush on Mount Horeb and said to him, "I have surely seen the affliction of my people which are in Egypt, and have heard their cry... I am come down to deliver them ...and to bring them up out of that land unto a good land... unto a land flowing with milk and honey " (Exodus 3:7,8). Moses and Aaron said to Pharaoh, "Thus saith the LORD God of Israel, Let my people go, that they may hold a feast unto me in the wilderness" (Exodus 5:1). At the end of ten plagues, Pharaoh released the Israelites from his grip, and they were free to go and worship God on the same mountain where God had earlier met with Moses.

After they had entered The Promised Land, the Israelites continued to sin against God, and so God sent them on exile into Babylon. When their captors said, "Sing us one of the songs of Zion" (Psalm 137:3), they replied, "How shall we sing the LORD's song in a strange land?" (v 4). Are we at the right place to serve and worship God today?

Jesus set free a woman, bent eighteen years by a spirit of infirmity; she straightened up and glorified God. (Luke 13:10-17). The woman's posture conveys significant truth: the weight of sin or oppression will bend spirits low, but when set free, they shall rise to praise God. The talent of singing misleads many to think highly of themselves or the other way around, others to think highly of the talented. It is the spirit that matters. God can be praised and worshipped at all times: morning, noon, evening or night by hearts which are in harmony with God. I have sung many times with Sunday school children,

> Praise Him, praise Him
> Praise Him in the morning,
> Praise Him in the noontime
> Praise Him, praise Him
> Praise Him when the sun goes down

(Praise Him, Praise Him, n.d.)

Praising is not the same as singing; we cannot sing while at work or asleep, but night or day, asleep or awake, the heart can always praise and worship God. How often we sing and pray with our lips while the heart is far from God! Worship must involve the whole: body, mind and spirit.

**Worship to be liberated**

Paul and Silas were singing and praising when in prison. Irrespective of where they were, they worshipped God. When the Israelites found it hard to sing the LORD's song in a strange land, how could Paul and Silas sing in prison? They knew the stone was rolled away from the mouth of the tomb and Paul had encountered the risen Lord Jesus. God set them free in a similar manner -a violent earthquake shook the foundations of the prison, and the prison doors opened. They led the keeper of the prison to faith in Christ, and they too were saved; the magistrates released Paul and Silas, and the prison-keeper said to Paul, "depart, and go in peace" (Acts 16:36). After they were set free, they went about liberating others.

**True worship**

There is a progression in Scripture: from bondage to freedom to worship the LORD, and worship when in bondage, to freedom to liberate others. To experience the liberation of one's spirit and free others with the truth: that is true worship.

❀ ❀ ❀

# The Master's Voice

*"My sheep hear my voice, and I know them, and they follow me: And I give unto them eternal life..." (John 10:27, 28)*

Adam and Eve heard God's voice in the garden of Eden and even had a conversation with Him. Failure to obey God's command led to their banishment, and their conversation ended. Out of love for humankind, God pursues and woos us back into the garden. "Thou that dwellest in the gardens, the companions hearken to thy voice: cause me to hear it" (Song of Solomon 8:13).

The LORD is in the garden of our hearts, calling for us and waiting to hear us. If we have listened to the LORD and obeyed, we can experience life in the garden and converse with Him once again.

## Through His servant Samuel

When the LORD called Samuel while he was asleep in the Temple where he ministered unto the LORD, the priest Eli who was also there did not hear. But when Samuel told him that he heard someone call his name, Eli knew that it was the LORD and taught him how to reply. Samuel answered, "Speak; for thy servant heareth" (1 Samuel 3:10), unlike the Israelites who said, "let not God speak with us, lest we die" (Exodus 20:19). Eli heard the LORD's judgment against his family, through Samuel who "grew before the LORD" (1 Samuel 2:21) and "was in favour both with the LORD, and also with men" (v26).

## Through the slave girl

Naaman's slave was a young girl from Israel. She saw that her master had leprosy. She knew about the prophet Elisha who had done miracles in Israel, and told her mistress that if Naaman could see Elisha, he would cure him of this disease. Naaman went to Elisha. Elisha did not come out but sent the message through his messenger: "Go and wash in Jordan seven times...and thou shalt be clean" (2 Kings 5:10). Naaman, though initially hesitant, later did what Elisha had told him to do, which cured him of leprosy. Naaman heard the LORD through the slave girl, the prophet Elisha and his messenger, and obedience brought about healing! He who could not stand in the presence of the LORD because of his uncleanness was now clean.

**Through His servant Israel**

Jesus is the LORD's chosen servant Israel; Israel serves both God and man. Jesus said to His disciples, "For even the Son of man came not to be ministered unto, but to minister..." (Mark 10:45). A man named Jairus sought Jesus when his daughter was dying. Before Jesus could get there, a servant from Jairus' house came saying, "Thy daughter is dead" (Mark 5:35). Jesus went with Jairus to his house; "And he took the damsel by the hand, and said unto her, Tăl'i-tha cū'mĭ; which is, being interpreted, Damsel, I say unto thee, arise. And straightway the damsel arose, and walked" (Mark 5:41,42). Jesus says, "...the dead shall hear the voice of the Son of God: and they that hear shall live" (John 5:25). "God... spake in time past unto the fathers by the prophets. Hath in these last days spoken unto us by His Son..." (Hebrews 1:1,2): The Master's Voice!

"The voice of the LORD is upon the waters...is powerful... full of majesty...breaketh the cedars...divideth the flames of fire...shaketh the wilderness...maketh the hinds to calve, and discovereth the forests..." (Psalm 29:3-9). Even the wind and the waves hear their Master's voice and obey! (Matthew 8:26).

God speaks today through The Bible. It is by faith in Christ Jesus that we shall hear the LORD, and enjoy pleasant conversations with Him in the garden of our souls.

## The Master's Voice

After the apostle Peter was miraculously freed from the prison, he went to Mary, the mother of John (also known as Mark). He knocked at the door, and a servant girl named Rhoda heard. She *knew* Peter's voice and immediately ran (without opening the door) to tell others that Peter was at the door. (Acts 12:14)

Jesus says, "Behold, I stand at the door, and knock: if any man hear my voice, and open the door, I will come in to him, and will sup with him, and he with me" (Revelation 3:20). Do we *know* The Master's voice?

❈ ❈ ❈

# Repent, Return, Receive, and Become

*"And rend your heart...and turn unto the LORD your God..." (Joel 2:13)*

The day of the LORD is near. It is time for all hearts to return to the LORD; He is waiting to bless and satisfy our souls.

## Repent

The human heart, by nature is sinful. The atonement for sin is sacrifice and offering to the LORD. Prophet Joel describes the destruction of the land of Judah: worms and locusts have invaded and ruined the fields, all the trees of the field are withered, the harvest destroyed, and the vine is dried up. People could make neither meat, nor grain, nor drink offering to the LORD (Joel 1:8-12). The prophet says greater destruction will come in the day of the LORD. So, he sends forth a call to repentance.

False prophets, false teachers, and false shepherds have invaded God's land like locusts. They allow neither grain to come forth out of the land nor fruit from the vine. It is a sure sign that the day of the LORD is near. In times of spiritual famine, what do we have to offer to the LORD?

## Return

The LORD says, "Turn ye even to me with all your heart, and with fasting, and with weeping, and with mourning" (Joel 2:12). If we do, "Who knoweth if he will return and repent, and leave a blessing behind him; even a meat offering and a drink offering..." (v 14). When mankind repents of sin and turns to God, God also repents of the destruction He has allowed, and returns with blessing, saying, "Behold, I will send you corn, and wine, and oil, and ye shall be satisfied..." (v19). Then there will be plenty to offer to the LORD.

## Receive

Jesus is the firstfruit, the perfect grain and drink offering to the LORD. In partaking of The Lord's Table, we share with Jesus, His life and become a kind of firstfruits for the LORD. Jesus said, "Except a corn of wheat fall into the ground and die, it abideth alone: but if it die, it bringeth forth much fruit" (John 12:24). Spiritual life is a sacrificial but fruitful life to be lived on earth, not to be reserved for heaven.

Jesus came to transform the natural into spiritual beings. Jesus said, "Ye must be born again" (John 3:7). Man is born again when his spirit is set free to reign over his body. Faith becomes the breath of a spiritual being. Many Christians give up carnal desires during the season of Lent and read more of The Word of God; the time spent in the Word must be fruitful, bringing to new birth. Natural man lives for God, whereas the spiritual man lives by the life of God. Death of self and receiving the life of Christ is a prerequisite for fruitful Christian ministry.

False religious leaders who have risen in fame but not in faith are sure to fall. Their fall will be so great that all nations will shudder! Jesus says, "Ye shall know them by their fruits" (Matthew 7:16). St. Paul lists works of the flesh: "Adultery, fornication, uncleanness, lasciviousness... drunkenness, revellings..." (Galatians 5:19–21). Works of faith are the fruit of the Spirit: "love, joy, peace, long-suffering, gentleness, goodness, faith, meekness, temperance" (Galatians 5:22, 23). Jesus asks, "For what shall it profit a man, if he shall gain the whole world, and lose his own soul? Or what shall a man give in exchange for his soul?" (Mark 8: 36, 37).

## Become

Every individual must work toward new birth so that in the day of the LORD and in times of spiritual famine, every soul will be a storehouse of grain and a vat overflowing with wine and oil. Repent and return to God; receive Christ the blessing and become an offering- a living sacrifice to the LORD.

\* \* \*

# Two To One

*"Be ye reconciled to God" (2 Corinthians 5:20)*

Mathematically, taking one away from two makes one, but adding one to two leads to reconciliation.

**Joseph and his brothers**

Jacob had a special place for his son Joseph, one of his twelve sons. The brothers plotted to kill Joseph but ultimately sold him to Egyptian merchants. Jealousy led to Joseph's separation from his brothers. Nevertheless, God raised Joseph to the highest position in Egypt, and when famine struck the land of Canaan, the time was ripe for reconciliation. The wise King Solomon writes, "To everything there is a season...a time to break down and a time to build up" (Ecclesiastes 3:1-3).

Famine brought the brothers to Joseph, and forgiveness mended the broken relationship and made them one again. From the life of Joseph, we can be sure that God will bring about something at the right time that will bind broken pieces together. Forgiveness reconciles one another.

**Heaven and Earth**

Heaven seems so far from earth. How shall they become one? The psalmist writes, "Mercy and truth are met together, righteousness and peace have kissed each other" (Psalm 85:10). Mercy, truth, righteousness and peace are of heaven; God shares them with the earth, in His Son Jesus Christ. The psalmist also says, "righteousness shall look down from heaven" (v 11), but will righteousness find peace on earth? Yes, "being justified by faith, we have peace with God through our Lord Jesus Christ" (Romans 5:1). Faith in Jesus Christ reconciles heaven and earth.

## Creator and Creation

In the wedding at Cana in Galilee, there arose a situation - no wine at the feast, when Jesus performed the first miracle: He made the water wine (John 2:1-11).

By the Word of God were all things in heaven and earth created. Therefore, the Creator can transform the created according to His need and purpose, provided the created yields to the Creator. Transformation is a sign of reconciliation. Total surrender and obedience to the Word reconciles Creator and creation.

## Jew and Gentile

Circumcision separates a Jew from a Gentile. The apostle Paul writes that "before faith came, we were kept under the law...but after that faith is come, we are no longer under a schoolmaster" (Galatians 3:23-25). Law required circumcision of God's people; faith also requires a kind of circumcision, not outward but inward "circumcision... of the heart" (Romans 2:29).

Before Christ, a Gentile had no hope of eternal life. But in Christ, "[t]here is neither Jew nor Greek, there is neither bond nor free, there is neither male nor female: for ye are all one in Christ Jesus" (Galatians 3:28). Christ reconciles Jew and Gentile, "to make in himself of twain one new man, so making peace" (Ephesians 2: 15).

## Man and God

Man is reconciled to God when forgiven at the Cross of Christ, justified by faith in Christ, and transformed into Christ's likeness by total surrender and obedience to His Word.

❋ ❋ ❋

# Know, Understand, and Do

*"Even a child is known by his doings, whether his work be pure, and whether it be right." (Proverbs 20:11)*

God's children ought to be righteous and pure.

**Know**

God gives us good counsel through His Word. "Counsel in the heart of man is like deep water; but a man of understanding will draw it out" (Proverbs 20:5). Knowledge and understanding are different. Reading the Word is knowledge; reading through the Word is understanding. For example, knowing there is water in the well is knowledge; understanding is drawing water from the well and drinking it to quench one's thirst. "The LORD giveth wisdom: out of His mouth cometh knowledge and understanding" (Proverbs 2:6). Read The Bible and know the Word.

**Understand**

To understand is to see through the pages of Scripture. The Holy Spirit gives us understanding, which is seeing Christ through The Word. In a world where sin is rampant, how shall this be?

Jesus, the Son of God, came to redeem and bring humankind into the way of righteousness. In the Garden of Gethsemane, Jesus' countenance was sad, and He prayed, "Father, if thou be willing, remove this cup from me: nevertheless not my will, but thine, be done" (Luke 22:42). The sinless Son of God drank of the sins of the world or works of the flesh [doings without understanding]:

"[a]dultery, fornication, uncleanness, lasciviousness... witchcraft, hatred, variance, emulations, wrath, strife, seditions, heresies... revellings and such like..." (Galatians 5:19-21), and died. He rose again so that, those called by God, may through faith in Him, bear the fruit of righteousness. Faith is the victory! Faith leads to righteousness and holiness (purity), without which we shall not see God. Jesus rose again and is seated at the right hand of God the Father. In His last discourse, Jesus said to His disciples, "ye are clean through the word which I have spoken unto you" (John 15:3); then, on the day of Pentecost, they received the Holy Spirit. What the apostles did later was done by the Holy Spirit, right and pure! Cleansing precedes Pentecost.

The apostle Paul writes, "...yield your members servants to righteousness unto holiness" (Romans 6:19) and "everlasting life" (v22), and not to sin, "for the end of those things is death" (v21). "Abraham believed God, and it was counted unto him for righteousness" (Romans 4:3). Jesus said, "...ye believe in God, believe also in me" (John 14:1). Even today, God speaks, cleanses by His Word, and baptizes with the Holy Spirit. Read 'through' the Word and understand.

## Do

Do the right things. The Pharisees believed that tithing made them righteous, but Jesus said, "these [judgment, mercy and faith] ought ye to have done, and not to leave the other [tithing] undone" (Matthew 23:23). By doing the two, we shall love both God and neighbour.

Christ in us will do the right things through us. Jesus said, "Ye shall know them [children of God] by their fruits...every good tree bringeth forth good fruit" (Matthew 7:16,17). Works without faith are no fruit, but works of faith in Christ Jesus are fruit of the Spirit, borne by the children of God. Do we have good fruit for heaven's Table? When the Lord returns, will there be a cup of righteousness to make His countenance glad?

St. Paul writes, "...I count all things but loss for the excellency of the knowledge of Christ Jesus my Lord...that I may win Christ. And be found in him not having mine own righteousness, which is of the law, but that which is through the faith of Christ, the righteousness which is of God by faith" (Philippians 3:8,9). Read, read through the Word, and do what is right and pure.

✳ ✳ ✳

# Water and Spirit

*"Is anything too hard for the LORD?" (Genesis 18:14)*

Can a barren womb bear children? Can a man be born again? "... with God nothing shall be impossible" (Luke 1:37).

## Blessing

Abram and Sarai were advanced in age when God said that many nations and kings would arise from him. Abram replied, "to me thou hast given no seed" (Genesis 15:3), and God said unto Abraham, "As for Sarai thy wife...I will bless her, and she shall be a mother of nations...Abram fell upon his face, and laughed, and said in his heart, Shall a child be born unto him that is an hundred years old? and shall Sarah, that is ninety years old, bear?" (Genesis 17:15-17). It is for the fulfilment of the promise that God gave Abraham a son; Abraham did not ask for a son but just made it known to God that he did not have an heir to inherit God's promised inheritance. Did God not know that Abraham had no son? God knows all things. We often ask God for what is outside of His will and purpose and are disappointed when not granted. But if something is necessary to fulfil God's purpose, we should make it known to Him, and He will give it. All it takes is a blessing from the LORD for the impossible to happen.

## Fruit

The LORD blessed Adam and Eve with these words: "Be fruitful and multiply" (Genesis 1:28). Children are the fruit of marriage. Unless the LORD blesses, the marriage will not be fruitful. In the spiritual life also, the priest pronounces the blessing at baptism with water, but it is the LORD who blesses and brings to fruit-bearing. The fruit of spiritual consummation is new birth.

Spiritual children are heirs of the inheritance. Jesus says, "the good seed are the children of the kingdom" (Matthew 13:38). Jesus also says, "I am the vine, ye are the branches: He that abideth in me, and I in him, the same bringeth forth much fruit: for without me you can do nothing" (John 15:5). Jesus has made it clear that not every branch that is in Him will bear fruit; the Father, who is the husbandman, will cut down such branches (John 15:2). The fruit of union with Christ is baptism with the Holy Spirit.

A man named Onesimus was a slave to Philemon, a Church leader at Colosse. He runs away from Philemon, meets the apostle Paul and becomes a Christian. The apostle Paul writes to Philemon, "in time past [Onesimus] was to thee unprofitable, but now profitable to thee and to me," and "not now as a servant... a brother beloved... both in the flesh, and in the LORD?" (Philemon v 11,16). As a natural man born of water, Onesimus was a slave to Philemon, but when born of the Spirit to faith in Jesus Christ, he becomes a spiritual brother in the LORD.

Every human being is carnal, for all are born of water, but those born of the Spirit become spiritual. The spiritual are subject to God and a brother to every one in faith. God's command to humankind is to love Him and one another; for this purpose, He will bring us to new birth, anytime and at any age. He will make the impossible possible! Born of water and Spirit, we shall love and serve both God and neighbour.

## Return

The LORD who has blessed will return at the appointed time to find fruit in that which He has blessed, just as He said He would return to find Sarah with a son. The LORD's return is imminent. Will He find heirs to His kingdom when He comes?

✻ ✻ ✻

# The Tree of Life

*"And out of the ground made the Lord God to grow every tree that is pleasant to the sight, and good for food; the tree of life also in the midst of the garden, and the tree of knowledge of good and evil" (Genesis 2: 9)*

The first man Adam and the woman Eve were given to enjoy the cool shades and the fruits of the trees in the garden of Eden but were commanded not to eat the fruit of the tree or touch the tree in the middle. If they touched, they would die (Genesis 3:3). However, they were soon driven out of the garden, away from God, because Eve ate of the forbidden tree, giving some to Adam. The fruit of the tree of knowledge of good and evil revealed that they were naked, without the divine garment of good. Out of His love for humanity, God has paved the way to be clothed again, get back into paradise, eat of the tree of life and live forever (Revelation 2:7).

## Trees of Pride

A tree in the middle of the land is an analogy to a King and his nation on earth. Kings and nations can either be rooted in God and grow tall, giving glory to Him forever, or be rooted in the serpent, giving glory to Satan, only to fall in the end.

"How art thou fallen from heaven, O Lucifer ...how art thou cut down to the ground which didst weaken the nations! For thou hast said in thine heart..., I will ascend above the heights of the clouds; I will be like the most High" (Isaiah 14: 12-14). "...it was through Pride that the devil became the devil: Pride leads to every other vice: it is the complete anti-God state of mind," writes C.S. Lewis (*Mere Christianity*, p.122).

The Kings of Assyria, the Pharaohs of Egypt and the Kings of Babylon were rooted in the serpent, and they grew into tall cedars of pride, bearing fruits of all kinds of evil. God spoke through the prophet Ezekiel that Pharaoh, even though tall, stately and majestic, would be hewn down and his branches strewn; his fall would be like that of the King of Assyria, so great, that nations around would shake. Pharaoh was felled never to rise again.

King Nebuchadnezzar of Babylon saw in a dream "...a tree in the midst of the earth, the height thereof reached unto heaven... the leaves thereof were fair and the fruit thereof much... an holy one came down from heaven...and said thus, Hew down the tree, and cut off his branches, shake off his leaves, and scatter his fruit...leave the stump of his roots in the earth" (Daniel 4: 10-15). Daniel interpreted this dream, thus: "It is thou O King that art grown and become strong: for thy greatness is grown, and reacheth unto heaven, and thy dominion to the end of the earth... thy kingdom shall be sure unto thee, after that thou shalt have known that the heavens do rule" (v 22, 26).

Daniel then gave his counsel to the King, "...break off thy sins by righteousness, and thine iniquities by shewing mercy to the poor" (v 27). Soon "there fell a voice from heaven, saying, O King Nebuchadnezzar...The kingdom is departed from thee... thy dwelling shall be with the beasts of the field: they shall make thee to eat grass as oxen..." (v 31, 32). Nebuchadnezzar did repent and humbled himself when The King of heaven and earth restored to him not only his kingdom but gave him new life [from beast to King] as well.

Herod, King of Judaea, was smitten by the angel of the Lord, soon after he made an oration to the people of Tyre and Sidon, "because he gave not God the glory" when the people shouted, "It is the voice of a god, and not of a man" (Acts 12: 21-23). Trees of pride are sure to fall.

**The Tree of Humility**

From a humble beginning as a shepherd boy, David was exalted to being King of Israel and blessed by God with the greatest blessing, "...thy kingdom shall be established forever before thee: thy throne shall be established forever" (2 Samuel 7:16). God spoke through the prophets, "...I will raise unto David a righteous Branch, and a King shall reign... in the earth" (Jeremiah 23:5); "And there shall come forth a rod out of the stem of Jesse [father of David], and a Branch shall grow out of his roots: and the spirit of the Lord shall rest upon Him..." (Isaiah 11: 1, 2).

The lowly birth of Jesus as an offshoot from the stump, His life of meekness, always acknowledging the Father in heaven and obedience unto a humiliating death on the Cross, makes Him the Tree of Humility. He grew not by His strength but by the strength of God the Father, fulfilling not His own but the Father's will. The Holy Spirit came upon Him, who is both King and Priest of Israel. Although this Tree was felled [crucified] by men, He rose by the power of The Holy Spirit and lives forever in His Kingdom above.

"Wherefore God also hath highly exalted Him, and given Him a name which is above every name: that at the name of Jesus every knee shall bow, of things in heaven, and things in earth, and things under the earth; and that every tongue should confess that Jesus Christ is Lord, to the glory of God the Father" (Philippians 2: 9-11).

Christ, the King, is the only tall, evergreen tree, firmly rooted as God, growing from earth to heaven, whose leaves will not wither and whose branches will bear luscious, good fruit. Upon Him, the birds can safely build their nests and raise their young, for there will be no wild beast to harm them there. The Tree of Humility can never fall.

**The Root**

A.W.Tozer asks, "If we do not know where we have been, how in the world are we going to determine where we are going...we look back so that we can make sure we are going forward in the right direction" (*The Dangers of a Shallow Faith*, A.W. Tozer p.20). Unless we know The Root, how can we know what fruit we will bear?

Faith of our fathers Abraham, Isaac, and Jacob and ancient Israel, as is known to us from the book of Genesis, takes us down to The Root of The Tree of Humility. The God whom they knew by the name God Almighty, later identifies Himself to Moses as, "... the God of Abraham, the God of Isaac and the God of Jacob.... name forever" (Exodus 3: 6, 15). The Lord said, "I appeared unto Abraham, unto Isaac, and unto Jacob, by the name God Almighty, but by my name JEHOVAH was I not known to them" (Exodus 6:3). JEHOVAH, the God of our fathers is The Root.

God called Abraham, set him on a journey, blessed his obedience, made a covenant with a promise of an inheritance, tested his faith, and established the covenant with Isaac. Isaac passed it on to Jacob. "The Lord, which stretcheth forth the heavens and layeth the foundation of the earth, and formeth the spirit of man within him" (Zechariah 12:1), formed Israel out of Jacob, from whom He brought forth a nation [the descendants of Jacob] and gave them The Promised Land for an inheritance. God took root among His people Israel, and out of this ground made the Lord God grow the tree of faith.

Israel, seeing their neighbouring nations ruled by kings, wanted a human king to rule over them. By seeking a human King, they rejected the Lord Almighty, The King of all the earth, who led them in their journey to the Promised Land and fought for them in all their battles, and now was in their midst. God did grant them their desire and anointed kings. If the King and his nation are rooted in the living God, and are worshipping Him in the Temple according to the Law, then the tree of faith will grow, but not when they reject God. Israel's sin became so great that the tree was felled, leaving only a stump. Israel was without a King and Temple; faith of our fathers could no longer grow. However, the Lord said, "I will be as the dew unto Israel..." (Hosea 14: 5). The hope of Israel's faith to sprout again is now in the Lord.

**The Branch**

"...Behold the man whose name is THE BRANCH and He shall grow up out of His place; and He shall build the temple of the Lord" (Zechariah 6:12). Jesus said, "Think not that I am come to destroy the law, or the prophets: I am not come to destroy, but to fulfil" (Matthew 5: 17). Christ fulfils the Law and the prophets. He is the King and the Temple. The birth, life, death, resurrection, and ascension of Jesus Christ paved the way for faith to grow. When the nation of Israel repents and turns to the Branch, acknowledging Jesus Christ as King, this shall be the blessing:

*"...he shall grow as the lily, and cast forth his roots as Lebanon. His branches shall spread, and his beauty shall be as the olive tree, and his smell as Lebanon. They that dwell under his shadow shall return; they shall revive as the corn, and grow as the vine...I [The Lord] am like a green fir tree. From me is thy fruit found." (Hosea 14: 5-8)*

"He shall cause them that come of Jacob to take root: Israel shall blossom and bud, and fill the face of the world with fruit" (Isaiah 27: 6).

None of the human kings or idol gods could save Israel and bring him to life except Jesus Christ. Job says, "If it [a tree] be cut down, that it will sprout again, and that the tender branch thereof will not cease. Though the root thereof wax old in the earth and the stock thereof die in the ground; yet through the scent of water it will bud, and bring forth boughs like a plant...If a man die, shall he live again? all the days of my appointed time will I wait, till my change come." (Job 14: 7- 9, 14). Where is the hope of man? His hope is in the Lord. Christ came not only to save Israel but all of humanity.

"Blessed is the man that trusteth in the Lord and whose hope the Lord is. For he shall be as a tree planted by the waters... her leaf shall be green...neither shall cease from yielding fruit" (Jeremiah 17: 7, 8).

Jesus saith, "It is the spirit that quickeneth... the words that I speak unto you, they are spirit and they are life" (John 6: 63). It is God who tills the ground [the spirit of man], quickens it and sows the seed [The Word] and rains on it dew from heaven "...faith cometh by hearing, and hearing by the Word of God" (Romans 10:17). Faith sprouts and grows into a tree rooted in God; this is God's handiwork. As faith grows, God reveals Himself to the spirit of man as in a mirror, "...dimly, but then face to face" (1 Corinthians 13:12), and man will find himself clothed with the garment of righteousness and revived by the life of God.

Such faith brought forth by God, will never die. *Faith of our fathers living still* a well-known hymn written by Frederick William Faber (1814-1863), affirms this. Jesus said, "I am the resurrection, and the life: he that believeth in me even though he were dead, yet shall he live: And whosoever liveth and believeth in me shall never die." (John 11:25, 26). "God is not a God of the dead but of the living: for all live unto Him" (Luke 20:38).

## The Fruit

Jesus saith, "I am Alpha and Omega, the beginning and the end, the first and the last" (Revelation 22:13). "...I am the root and the offspring of David..." (Revelation 22:16). Jesus Christ, who is The Branch is also The Root and The Fruit; He who is Humility, is also Strength and Power. The Fruit of the Tree of Humility is The Holy Spirit.

Jesus said to His disciples, "...I have chosen you, and ordained you, that ye should go and bring forth fruit, and that your fruit should remain..." (John 15:16). Jesus saith, "Abide in me, and I in you. As the branch cannot bear fruit of itself, except it abide in the vine; no more can ye, except ye abide in me. I am the vine, ye are the branches: He that abideth in me, and I in him, the same bringeth forth much fruit: for without me ye can do nothing" (John 15:4, 5).

The Holy Spirit came upon all who were waiting in Jerusalem after the ascension of Christ, anointing them into the royal priesthood as apostles, who would then go and make disciples "baptizing them in the name of the Father, the Son and the Holy Spirit" (Matthew 28:19).

The apostles proclaimed the message: "Repent and be baptized ..." (Acts 2:38), and they grafted many a gentile onto The Branch by baptism. Those grafted, remained in Him drawing strength from The Root and nourishment from the sap of the trunk until they died to self and by faith, became one with Christ saying, "... not I, but Christ liveth in me..." (Galatians 2:20). Death of self leaves no room for pride but for Humility to grow; "He must [will] increase, but I [the graft] must [will] decrease" (John 3: 30). Apart from Christ, no man can grow in humility. Jesus calls us not to enjoy His shade but to grow into Him and bear fruit.

John the Baptist said, "I baptize you with water unto repentance... He [Jesus] will baptize you with the Holy Ghost, and with fire" (Matthew 3:11). Man only grafts; the graft must allow himself to be taken up into Christ and receive the Holy Spirit. He will then be empowered to go and bear fruit; faith will now bear fruit. Jesus prayed, "that they [his disciples and all who will believe in Him, through their message] all may be one...as thou Father art in me and I in thee, that they also may be one in us..." (John 17: 20, 21). By faith, man becomes one with God; all such men will indeed be one, for they will all be branches of The One Tree.

A branch without fruit is faith without works; it is dead. Jesus warns that the Father will cut down such branches. Jesus cursed the fig tree that was without fruit, and it dried up from the root. When the disciples asked him about this, Jesus said, "Have faith in God" (Mark 11:22). A. W. Tozer writes, "The tree does not serve in lieu of fruit but as an agent by which fruit is secured. Fruit, not trees, is the end God has in mind in yonder orchard; so Christ like conduct is the end of Christian faith." (*Of God and Men*, A.W. Tozer p.61) In today's Christian world, we are in a hurry to bear fruit. "Our fathers looked well to the root of the tree and were willing to wait with patience for the fruit to appear. We demand the fruit immediately even though the root may be weak and knobby or missing altogether," writes A.W. Tozer (The *Root of the Righteous* A. W. Tozer p. 7). Has our faith taken root in the living God?

God is triune; it is, therefore, right to describe our faith in Him as Judeo - Christian - Apostolic, not to be separated, but to be lived and enjoyed whole. A true Christian [individual, family or nation] will be humble, yet strong and powerful like his God.

## Christ - The Tree of Life

Christ's nation on earth is the Church, and His Kingdom is heaven above, "and of His kingdom there shall be no end" (Luke 1:33). Jesus saith, "The kingdom of heaven is like to a grain of mustard seed, which a man took and sowed in his field: Which indeed is the least of all seeds: but when it grows it is the greatest among herbs, and becometh a tree..." (Matthew 13: 31,32) and "... the kingdom of God is within you" (Luke 17:21). When faith grows tall, heaven comes down and fills the soul of man. Jesus saith, "To him that overcometh [world's temptations, by faith], will I give to eat of the Tree of Life which is in the paradise of God" (Revelation 2:7). Also, "...they that do His commandments ...have right to the tree of life, that they may enter in through the gates into the city" (Revelation 22:14).

May every man be blessed to say, "And out of the ground (my spirit) made the Lord God to grow faith in Christ - The Tree of Life, by which I shall take flight to paradise and eat of the Fruit and live forever!"

## References

Lewis, C. S. *Mere Christianity: A Revised and Amplified    Edition.* New York: HarperCollins Publishers, 2001. 122. Print

Tozer. A. W. *The Dangers of a Shallow Faith.* Compiled and Edited by James L. Snyder. California: Regal, 2012. 20. Print (Tozer 1989)

Tozer. A. W. *Of God and Men.* Maharashtra, India: Alliance Publications, 1989. 61. Print

Tozer. A.W. *The Root of the Righteous*. Maharashtra, India: Alliance Publications, 1989. 7. Print

✻ ✻ ✻

# The Cupbearer

*"I was the king's cupbearer" (Nehemiah 1:11)*

In ancient days, the cupbearer would serve drinks, usually wine, to the King. The King would choose a trustworthy man for this purpose, one who would be willing to taste the drink before serving it, though it might cost him his life while protecting the King from tainted glasses. It is proper etiquette that the cupbearer enter the King's presence with a joyful countenance; only then would the King take the cup, and his heart would be made glad, and both would live. On the other hand, if the cupbearer's countenance were sad, the King would not take the cup, which implied the cupbearer would have to taste the drink and risk his life.

## Pharaoh's cupbearer

The Pharaoh's chief butler ("cupbearer" in New International Version) and baker were with Joseph in prison. The two of them had dreams which they shared with Joseph.

The cupbearer said, "In my dream, behold, a vine was before me; And in the vine were three branches: and it was as though it budded, and her blossoms shot forth; and the clusters thereof brought forth ripe grapes: And Pharaoh's cup was in my hand: and I took the grapes, and pressed them into Pharaoh's cup, and I gave the cup into Pharaoh's hand. And Joseph said unto him... [t]he three branches are three days: Yet within three days shall Pharaoh lift up thine head, and restore thee unto thy place: and thou shalt deliver Pharaoh's cup into his hand, after the former manner when thou wast his butler. But think on me when it shall be well with thee, and make mention of me unto Pharaoh, and bring me out of this house" (Genesis 40: 9-14).

The baker said, "behold, I had three white baskets on my head. And in the uppermost basket there was of all manner of bakemeats for Pharaoh; and the birds did eat them out of the basket upon my head. And Joseph answered and said… [t]he three baskets are three days: Yet within three days shall Pharaoh lift up thy head from off thee, and shall hang thee on a tree; and the birds shall eat thy flesh from off thee" (Genesis 40:16-19). And so it happened. "Yet did not the chief butler remember Joseph, but forgat him" (v 23).

Two years later, when Pharaoh had a dream that needed interpretation, the cupbearer remembered Joseph. The Pharaoh shared his dream with Joseph and Joseph, saying, "It is not in me: God shall give Pharaoh an answer of peace," (Genesis 41:16) interpreted it. The Pharaoh recognized the Spirit of God in Joseph and said: "Thou shalt be over my house, and according unto thy word shall all my people be ruled: only in the throne will I be greater than thou" (Genesis 41:40).

## Nehemiah the cupbearer

While the prophet Nehemiah was cupbearer to King Artaxerxes of Persia, he was told, "the remnant that are left of the captivity… are in great affliction and reproach: the wall of Jerusalem also is broken down, and the gates thereof are burned with fire" (Nehemiah 1:3). Nehemiah "sat down and wept, and mourned…and fasted, and prayed before the God of heaven" for "mercy in the sight of [the king]" (v 4, 11).

When he took the cup to the King, the King asked, "Why is thy countenance sad, seeing thou art not sick? this is nothing else but sorrow of heart" (Nehemiah 2:2). Nehemiah said to him, "Let the King live forever: why should not my countenance be sad, when the city, the place of my fathers' sepulchres lieth waste, and the gates…consumed with fire?" (v 3). Then the King said, "For what dost thou make request?" So [Nehemiah] prayed to the God of heaven. And [he] said to the King, "If it please the king, and if thy servant have found favour in thy sight...send me unto Judah, unto the city of my fathers' sepulchres, that I may build it" (v 4, 5). The King granted his request, and Nehemiah set out to Jerusalem to inspect the wall and the gate and then told the Jews, the priests, the nobles, the rulers and the rest, "let us build up the wall of Jerusalem, that we be no more a reproach...And they said, Let us rise up and build. So they strengthened their hands for this good work" (v 17, 18).

Although Nehemiah's hands bore a cup of wine to the King, his heart was a cup of prayer, raised to the King of heaven and earth; a cup filled with confession of the sins of Israel, and requests for God's forgiveness and strength to rebuild the broken walls and fortify the city. God did drink of this cup and in return filled it with heaven's blessings through the hand of the earthly King. Wine made the King's heart glad, whereas Nehemiah's heart gladdened with heaven's blessings. After Nehemiah rebuilt the wall, and the people gathered to listen to the Book of the Law, he said to them, "mourn not, nor weep... for the joy of the LORD is your strength" (Nehemiah 8: 9,10). The Law and the Prophets point to Christ and His Kingdom.

## The Father's Cupbearer

Jesus grieved over the spiritual brokenness of His Father's world. He bore a cup of sorrow, of the fruits of earth's vine (the sins of the world) while in the Garden of Gethsemane. He kneeled, and prayed saying, "Father, if thou be willing, remove this cup from me: nevertheless not my will, but thine be done" (Luke 22:42) The Father, however, did not take the cup from Him. Jesus had to drink of this cup and die. He became the winepress of the Father's wrath, out of which would flow 'blood'. He died on the Cross but was lifted from the grave unto glorious resurrection in three days, and restored to His place in the Father's House. The sentences pronounced by Pharaoh upon the baker and cupbearer were upon the Son of God. However, the Father's cupbearer will no longer die but forever live with Him, seated at His right hand, interceding for His disciples, unlike the Pharaoh's cupbearer who forgot to intercede for Joseph.

During the last supper, "[Jesus] took the cup, and gave thanks, and gave it to [His disciples], saying, Drink ye all of it; For this is my blood of the new testament, which is shed for many for the remission of sins" (Matthew 26: 28). He also said, "Except ye eat the flesh of the Son of man, and drink his blood, ye have no life in you" (John 6:53) and "He that eateth my flesh, and drinketh my blood, dwelleth in me, and I in him" (v 56). By His life alone, we shall bear the fruit of heaven's Vine. Jesus said, "For even the Son of Man came not to be ministered unto but to minister..." (Mark 10:45). He serves Himself to us in the sacrament of Eucharist; He is the bread and wine of heaven. After such great love, if we should still bear bad fruit, who can save us? "The angel thrust in his sickle into the earth, and gathered the vine of the earth, and cast it into the great winepress of the wrath of God" (Revelation 14:19).

Jesus said, "I will not drink henceforth of this fruit of the vine, until that day when I drink it new with you in my Father's kingdom" (Matthew 26:29). How long shall we eat and drink of the Lord's Table and not bear fruit for heaven's table? The earth's vine will only bring sorrow and eternal death, whereas heaven's vine shall bring forth gladness and everlasting life. Jesus said, "I AM the true vine, and my Father is the husbandman" (John 15:1). As in the wedding at Cana, the best is for the end.

If the Father's heart is made glad by the fruit of the true vine, He will pour a cup full of blessing on us and make our hearts joyful in return. Do we have good fruit? The Father also hath in His hand the cup of indignation; if He should pour of it on us, we are sure to die. Jesus said to His disciples, "I have chosen you, and ordained you, that ye should go and bring forth fruit, and that your fruit should remain: that whatsoever ye shall ask of the Father in my name, he may give it you" (John 15:16). Let us drink of the cup of the New Testament, bear good fruit, and receive the Father's blessing.

Nehemiah together with the Jews, rebuilt the broken wall and gates of Jerusalem. Out of the ruins of this world, Jesus together with His disciples, will build the heavenly city- The New Jerusalem.

\* \* \*

# Advent

*"And blessed is she that believed: for there shall be a performance of those things which were told her from the Lord" (Luke 1:45)*

Advent means 'coming'. God is faithful and true to His promises. We can be sure of the coming of His promises. God fulfilled the promise He made to Abraham in Israel. When the nation of Israel obeyed God, they enjoyed the peace and the light of God's presence, but when they disobeyed, they were taken captive by their enemies and were in darkness. When Judah and Jerusalem were desolate, "Behold, the days come, saith the LORD, that I will perform that good thing which I have promised unto the house of Israel and to the house of Judah" (Jeremiah 33:14). There will be sounds of joy and laughter, flocks grazing the fields, rejoicing of the bride and groom (v 10-13). We can hope for a similar blessing after the desolation of Churches and homes due to the COVID-19 pandemic, because the LORD has spoken it.

At a time of spiritual darkness, Israel's hope was in the Word of God: "Behold, a virgin shall conceive, and bear a son, and shall call his name Immanuel" (Isaiah 7:14). The prophet Isaiah writes of a voice in the wilderness calling for preparation before the coming of the Saviour:

> *"Prepare ye the way of the LORD, make straight in the desert a highway for our God. Every valley shall be exalted, and every mountain and hill shall be made low: and the crooked shall be made straight, and the rough places plain: And the glory of the LORD shall be revealed, and all flesh shall see it together: for the mouth of the LORD hath spoken it ." (Isaiah 40:3-5)*

## Jesus' birth

After a period of darkness came light! Mary was an ordinary Jewish girl on whom God's favour rested; she would conceive and bear a son- the Christ child, called Jesus. He is "that good thing" which the LORD promised. Mary went to see her cousin, Elizabeth, after the angel spoke to her and revealed what would happen to her. On seeing Mary, Elizabeth said, "And blessed is she that believed: for there shall be a performance of those things which were told her from the Lord" (Luke 1:45).

Mary's response to the situation (the Magnificat) was similar to Hannah's when she conceived Samuel. Mary saw herself as a lowly handmaiden, and her soul magnified the LORD. The humble human servant or vessel was *blessed* and *used* by God for His glory; the LORD alone is exalted and glorified. It is clear from Scripture, that God's favour rests: not on the proud, but the humble; not on the mountain, but the hill; not on the rich, but the poor, not on those filled, but the hungry. Great things shall come out of those on whom God's favour rests!

Elizabeth gave birth to John. To those who wanted to know who he was, John confessed, "I am not the Christ" (John 1:20), and said, "I am the voice of the one crying in the wilderness, [m]ake straight the way of the LORD, as said the prophet [Isaiah]" (v 23).

## Christ's birth

We celebrate Jesus' birth once every year, but Christ can be born many times, in many human hearts and many places. "And the Word was made flesh, and dwelt among us..." (John 1:14). The same Word is made Christ for us by the Holy Spirit, to dwell in our hearts and homes and Churches and nations. Mountains of pride must be brought low, and valleys of defeat raised, in anticipation of the birth of Christ. God chooses His dwelling place— the hill of the LORD. Mountains and hills surround Jerusalem; a lowly hill finds favour with God (Psalm 68:15,16). Let hearts and homes be lowly in His sight, so Christ shall be born there, before Jesus returns. Preparation for advent is the norm.

## Jesus' return

After much tribulation: wars, afflictions, famines, and pestilences, and earthquakes, much iniquity, false Christs, and false prophets (Matthew 24:7-24) and "the working of Satan" (2 Thessalonians 2:9), "the powers of the heavens shall be shaken" (Matthew 24:29) and Jesus shall come not as Saviour but as Judge. His coming shall be "as the lightning cometh out of the east, and shineth even unto the west" (v 27). He will come swiftly; no enemy can stop Him. The righteous shall rejoice, and the unrighteous will flee and scatter, for they cannot stand in the presence of a righteous God. How shall we prepare for the second advent or Jesus' return? "...he that is righteous, let him be righteous still: and he that is holy, let him be holy still" (Revelation 22:11).

Those who by faith believe the truth can hope for: The Promised Land after the wilderness, habitation after desolation, light after darkness, and after the tribulation- the coming of the Lord!

\* \* \*

# Potter, Pot, Purpose

*"Yea, every pot in Jerusalem and in Judah shall be holiness unto the LORD of hosts..."* (Zechariah 14:21)

The LORD is Creator. He made man (a pot) out of clay and breathed His life into him. Made by Holy Hands, Adam is holy to the LORD. God put him in the garden "to dress it and to keep it" (Genesis 2:15) and blessed saying, "[b]e fruitful and multiply" (Genesis 1:28). However, things did not go the way they had to. Adam sinned and so was unable to fulfil the purpose. The pot can serve its purpose only when the divine life is in it. How shall Adam's race which has lost that life, fulfil God's purpose? Today, we hear a lot about caring for the earth, but what about the garden? How shall we care for it?

## Return to the LORD

First of all, we must come back to The LORD's presence. For this purpose, God sent His only begotten [not made] Son Jesus into the world. Jesus said to His disciples, "Ye are not of the world, but I have chosen you out of the world" (John 15:19). Just as Jesus is not of this world, so are His disciples; they are people of the garden, called to bear fruit. Faith in Jesus Christ takes us into the presence of God and brings God to ours, and our hearts become the LORD's garden- a garden in a pot! Heaven and earth meet in the garden. When the heart is well-tended, out of the pot shall come forth fruit. The LORD is the Potter, and we are His handiwork; He is the Vinedresser, and we are the branches. Jesus said, "Without me ye can do nothing" (John 15:5). Without Christ, we can neither be moulded into the perfect pot nor tended to bear good fruit.

## In the Potter's Hands

The LORD formed Israel [a large pot] out of Jacob and gave them His Law. Israel was to obey the Law and be holy. Just as Adam failed, so did Israel. The Israelites were living away from God's presence in bondage under the Pharaoh of Egypt. The LORD chose Moses to redeem them and take them into The Promised Land where The LORD would be their God, and they would be His people, according to the covenant He made with Abraham. However, because of their repeated disobedience, God scattered them; one large pot now strewn as fragments all over.

Prophets repeatedly called the Israelites to return to The LORD. The LORD asked Jeremiah to go to the Potter's house, and there the LORD said, "O house of Israel...as the clay is in the potter's hand, so are ye in mine hand, O house of Israel" (Jeremiah 18:6). He could either mould and shape them into the pot He intends, or He could break them if they did not turn from their evil ways. (Jeremiah 18:7-11). Is it not good to remain in the Potter's hands until He is done with us and sets us down to be of use?

## The priceless Pot

In the prophet Zechariah's time, many false shepherds neither cared for the sheep nor allowed the sheep to enjoy the beauty of the LORD. They marked some sheep for slaughter and some for sale. Buyers paid the price for the sheep, and the shepherds boasted that they were now rich. The LORD asked Zechariah to shepherd the sheep marked for slaughter, with two staves: "Beauty" and "Bands" (Zechariah 11:7). Sadly, the sheep reject the shepherd, and so he breaks the staves. The breaking of "Beauty" meant, breaking of covenant between God and sheep, and the breaking of "Bands", breaking of fellowship among the sheep. (Zechariah 11:10,14)

The remnant which remains faithful to the LORD, He will "refine" and "try" (Zechariah 13:9) so every pot shall be "holiness unto the LORD of hosts..." (Zechariah 14:21). The LORD will bless them and "the seed shall be prosperous; the vine shall give her fruit, and the ground shall give her increase and the heavens shall give their dew..." (Zechariah 8:12).

Jesus, the Good Shepherd is foreshadowed in Zechariah. The Shepherd's care is free to those within the covenant. But after the covenant is broken, the shepherd says, "If ye think good, give me my price" (Zechariah 11:12), and they paid thirty pieces of silver, and the LORD said to Zechariah, "cast it unto the potter" (v 13). Judas Iscariot [doomed for destruction] priced Christ at thirty pieces of silver and betrayed Him. It must have grieved the LORD whose Christ the HOLY ONE OF ISRAEL is invaluable and priceless. While Adam is of clay, Christ is of the Word, "And the Word was made flesh, and dwelt among us..." (John 1:14). In Christ, the sheep can always enjoy the beauty of the LORD and fellowship with one another.

**Purpose**

It is over a sacrifice that God sealed the covenant with Abraham (Genesis 15:9-18). Jesus is the ultimate sacrifice for Adam's race; "the good shepherd giveth his life for the sheep" (John 10:11); the priceless Pot was broken for us. We must not reject Him if we should remain in covenant with God and in fellowship with one another. The Potter shall mould us [individuals, homes, Churches and nations] into pots that will hold the holy seed - the Word of God, so the seed may grow by the divine life of Christ to bear fruit, thereby fulfilling God's purpose: "[b]e fruitful and multiply and replenish the earth" (Genesis 1:28).

✽ ✽ ✽

# By His Hands

*"O LORD, Thou art our father; we are the clay and thou our potter; and we all are the work of thy hand" (Isaiah 64:8)*

God created a perfect man and woman and gave them a beautiful garden wherein to dwell with Him. The ideal pair soon became imperfect and unacceptable to remain in the presence of a perfect and holy God. Who shall stand in the sacred place and serve the LORD?

## Made adequate

The wholesome nurturing of a child includes caring for the body, mind, and spirit. Moses grew up in a palace with royal food and clothes. Yet, when God wanted him to speak to Pharaoh, Moses said, "O my Lord, I am not eloquent...I am slow of speech and of a slow tongue" (Exodus 4:10); He was inadequate to carry out God's will. Even when God said, "I will put words in your mouth...." Moses refused. God gave him a helper, his brother Aaron to speak just as a prophet would speak for God; in addition, God gave him a staff with which he could perform miracles (Exodus 4:10-17). God's giving is always bountiful. God did not choose a different leader but provided all the resources that Moses would need to lead Israel out of the clutches of the Pharaoh of Egypt. Scripture says, "And there arose not a prophet since in Israel like unto Moses, whom the LORD knew face to face" (Deuteronomy 34:10). Made adequate, Moses became instrumental in the fulfilment of God's promise to Israel.

## Made whole

Jesus healed a man paralyzed for thirty-eight long years and lying on a mat by the pool of Bethesda (John 5:1-15). Later at the temple, Jesus met him and said, "Sin no more..." (v 12). Made whole, this man evangelized to the Jews.

## Made strong

Where can we find the strength to do God's will? Jesus said, "...without me ye can do nothing" (John 15: 5). Yes, "[We] can do all things through Christ which strengtheneth [us]" ( Philippians 4:13). Between weakness and strength is a heart that is willing to be a vessel in His hands. The apostle Paul, God's chosen vessel was given "a thorn in the flesh, the messenger of Satan to buffet" (2 Corinthians 12:7) so he would not boast of his own strength. When he sought the Lord, that it might depart from him, the Lord said, "My grace is sufficient for thee: for my strength is made perfect in weakness" and the apostle says, "Most gladly therefore will I rather glory in my infirmities, that the power of Christ may rest upon me" (v 9). Made strong with Christ, the apostle Paul preached the Word to the Gentiles.

## By His hands

God moulds and shapes hearts placed in His hands: filling in inadequacies, making whole and strengthening with Christ, to fulfil His purposes.

❊ ❊ ❊

# King, Servant, Service

*"...the Son of Man came not to be ministered unto, but to minister, and to give his life a ransom for many" (Matthew 20:28)*

God is triune. Scripture shows Him as King, Servant and Service. The world knows that it is essential and good to serve others, but acts of the apostles of Christ are different from those of others. From the life of Jesus and His apostles, we see that godly acts are carried out by the Holy Spirit, for such acts convert hearts to the living God.

## King's favour

### Esther

Esther was an ordinary Jewish orphan girl raised by her cousin Mordecai. She became Queen of Persia, which King Xerxes ruled. A wicked high official in the palace plotted to kill all the Jews in the land, and Mordecai, who came to know of it, asked Esther to intercede for her people before the King. She approached the King without being summoned. She found favour with the King and saved the Jews. The queen humbled herself as a servant and served her people with life! A godly act! People of many nationalities became Jews, as they feared them who had found favour with the King. (Esther 8:17)

### Daniel

Daniel, a Hebrew captive in Babylon, feared the living God - the God of Abraham, the God of Isaac and the God of Jacob. He worshipped his God and prayed to Him regularly. King Darius made a law that stated that no one should pray to any god or man except the King. Daniel did not obey the law, and so he was thrown into the lion's den. God closed the mouths of the lions and saved Daniel. Early next morning the King saw that Daniel was unharmed. Daniel found favour with God the King, and so He blessed and served the earthly King who gave him a death sentence. A godly act indeed! for the King recognized that Daniel's God was the only true living God and ordered that his nation revered and worshipped Him. (Daniel 6: 1-26).

## Servant's humility

### Jesus

To the poor and needy, the LORD says, "now will I arise...I will set [you] in safety from him that puffeth at [you]" (Psalm 12:5). After four hundred long years from the end of the Old Testament times, the Son of God, came from heaven to earth to save God's people from Satan, sin, and death and give them eternal life! He took the servant nature and served God's people with compassion. He worked miracles, healed diseases, taught the simple, washed the feet of His disciples, died on the Cross and rose again by the power of the Holy Spirit. He did not claim to be the Father or the Holy Spirit, but through His birth, life, and death reveals them both, and in so doing, exemplifies humility.

## Godly service

### Apostles

Followers of Christ are children of the heavenly King; they are royal servants who must serve God's people with humility on earth until Jesus returns as King of kings and Lord of lords! They are people who have found favour with God through Christ. They can approach the King without being summoned because of what Christ has done for them and in them. The Spirit of Christ will lead them to do great acts of godly service to others. The book of Acts in The Bible is full of such service of the apostles of Christ, that is, making disciples. A true Christian will enjoy the King's favour, reveal the humility of Christ Jesus, and serve by the power of the Holy Spirit.

✻ ✻ ✻

# From Darkness to Glory!

*"He is not here..." (Matthew 28:6)*

Who can raise us from the depths of darkness to heights of glory above?

## Pit to Palace

Joseph, who found favour in his father's eyes, was thrown into a waterless cistern (a dark pit) by his jealous brothers and later sold to Ishmaelites, who took him to Egypt. God was with Joseph and raised him to the highest honour in this foreign land: from the pit to the palace!

When Jacob saw Joseph's robe, he said, "I will go down into the grave unto my son mourning" (Genesis 37:35) when in fact, Joseph was not in the grave but in a palace.

## Earth to Heaven

Jesus came from heaven to shed light and lift humankind from earth to heaven above. Jesus said to a rich man, "...go and sell that thou hast, and give to the poor, and thou shalt have treasure in heaven: and come and follow me" (Matthew 19:21). Joseph had no possessions when he entered Egypt but received the highest honour- a robe, a ring, and a palace. God leads us in such a way that when we inherit Christ, our material possessions automatically lose their grip on us, freeing us to make our upward journey.

Jesus, who is life and light, was crucified and buried in a dark tomb. The angels appeared to the women who were at the tomb looking for the body of Jesus and said to them, "Why seek ye the living among the dead? He is not here, but is risen" (Luke 24:5,6). Jesus was out in the garden, and Mary Magdalene thought He was "the gardener" (John 20:15). She was indeed right, for in Christ we see The Vinedresser, The Vine and The Fruit. The branches have nothing to boast about, except Christ. After His resurrection, Jesus appeared to His disciples and later ascended into heaven.

**Darkness to Glory**

Christ is the portal of light and life! A Christian need not mourn for the dead, for "the dead in Christ shall rise" (1 Thessalonians 4:16). St. Paul who knew Christ as the storehouse of heavenly riches, writes, "I count all things but loss for the excellency of the knowledge of Christ Jesus my LORD: for whom I have suffered the loss of all things, and do count them but dung, that I may win Christ" (Philippians 3: 8) and "Christ in [us] the hope of glory" (Colossians 1:27). When in Christ, we shall rise by the power of the Holy Spirit not only after death but also in life, from depths of darkness to glorious heights above!

* * *

# From Garden to Paradise!

*"Verily I say unto you, today shalt thou be with me in paradise"* (Luke 23:43)

Jesus made the above promise to one of the two criminals on the Cross. How refreshing that must have been to a dying soul! To make this promise good for us, we must understand the One who made the promise, and the man to whom He made it and respond accordingly.

**Garden**

"In the beginning God created the heaven and the earth" (Genesis 1:1). He made everything good. He made man in His image; He planted a garden and put Adam there "to dress it and to keep it" (Genesis 2:15), in other words, to tend the garden. There was the Tree of Life and a river that watered the garden. Sin led to Adam's fall; God banished him from the garden. We are by our natural birth - a sinful, fallen race, outside the garden, with a tarnished image, and our purpose lost. Humankind needs a Redeemer, Restorer and Saviour.

"For God so loved the world, that he gave his only begotten Son, that whosoever believeth in him should not perish, but have everlasting life" (John 3:16).

St. Paul refers to Jesus as "the last Adam or the second Man". He also writes, "the first man [Adam] is of the earth, earthy: the second man [or last Adam] is "the Lord from heaven" (Jesus Christ-The Word made flesh). The first Adam was made a living soul; the last Adam was made a quickening Spirit [or life-giving Spirit]" (1

Corinthians 15:45-49). The Spirit of Christ will quicken our faith and spirit so we may see 'the Christ' in Jesus and His Kingdom and be redeemed, restored and saved.

To be bought with a price is redemption, and the price is the life of our Lord; to become Christ-like is restoration or transformation, and to be saved from the second death for life in paradise is salvation.

**Cross**

Jesus, the sinless Son of God and two criminals were under the same sentence - death by crucifixion, which fulfils Isaiah's prophecy: "he was numbered with the transgressors" (Isaiah 53:12).

One man said to Jesus, "If thou be Christ, save thyself and us" (Luke 23:39). Firstly, this man doubted the divinity of Jesus. He wanted to see Jesus come down from the Cross and get him also out of there before he would believe that Jesus was the Christ, the Son of God. Secondly, he saw only life in this world and was blind to the Kingdom of heaven, which is beyond the Cross. Thirdly, to him, salvation meant coming down from the Cross and back in this world, free of suffering and pain. "If in this life only we have hope in Christ, we are of all men most miserable" writes St. Paul (1 Corinthians 15:19). Who can save us from the second death but Christ alone! The unrepentant criminal is to be pitied for Jesus neither spoke to him nor did He save him. He remained a natural man and died.

The other man rebuked the unrepentant criminal, saying, "Dost not thou fear God, seeing thou art under the same condemnation? And we indeed justly... but this man [Jesus] hath done nothing amiss" (Luke 23: 40,41). He saw how God spared not His own Son from death on the Cross. Christ suffered and died for our salvation. The world is suffering and is in great pain due to the COVID- 19 pandemic and its effects. The Cross assures that when suffering is great, salvation is near! We must fear God, a God who allows suffering and pain and death in everyone's life, just as "he maketh his sun to rise on the evil and on the good, and sendeth rain on the just and on the unjust" (Matthew 5:45) only to take away the good and the just to His Kingdom.

Every good thing follows the fear of the LORD. Without seeking a sign, the repentant man saw Jesus as the Christ by perfect faith, and in spirit saw His Kingdom beyond the Cross. He saw himself as deserving the suffering and pain of the Cross and death but knew that Jesus unjustly crucified would, after death, enter the Kingdom of heaven. Seeing the purity of Christ and His Kingdom, he saw himself unworthy of life in that Kingdom and knew that the two of them (Jesus and himself) would have to part ways on the other side of the Cross, and so he said, "Lord, remember me when thou comest into Thy kingdom" (Luke 23:42).

When friends part and bid farewell, and each one goes their way, they will say to one another, 'Remember me' or 'don't forget me'. When the man said to Jesus, "remember me", Jesus said, "Today shalt thou be with me..." (Luke 23:43). Such is the love of Jesus! Jesus is compassionate and generous. Love's response to faith of a repentant soul is the assurance of what faith hopes for – the salvation of the soul.

What the first Adam failed to give to the human race, Christ the last Adam gives! Christ restores the lost image and purpose in us. At the Cross, a criminal is truly born again and receives the assurance of paradise! This man has become Christ-like, pointing humanity to God; he is the first and the only man who preaches year after year from the Cross, the most important of all messages: Fear God; repent, the Kingdom of heaven is near. He continues the work of Christ even after his death. In a world where false teachers and preachers abound, here is one man truly converted. Once a criminal, now a preacher; once a natural man, now spiritual. We can trust him and his words. He found his purpose on the Cross.

Jesus while on earth said, "Repent: for the kingdom of heaven is at hand" (Matthew 4:17); "Except a man be born again, he cannot see the kingdom of God" (John 3:3), and from heaven said to the apostle John, "Behold, I make all things new" (Revelation 21:5). In the repentant criminal, all of these have come true. Christ has indeed redeemed, restored and saved this man for paradise!

## Heart

The two criminals represent two hearts. One fears God, sees itself sinful and undeserving of life in the Kingdom of heaven, perfectly believes that Jesus is the Christ, and rests its faith in Him. Another fears the evils and injustices of the world, doubts the divinity of Jesus, sees only this world, sees itself sinless and deserving a pain-free life in this world. How is ours? If we say we have no sin in us, we are taking the place of Jesus and making His death meaningless and in vain. God forbid.

We must put to death our sinful nature, so our hearts may become God's dwelling place. When Christ makes His dwelling in us, He will tend the garden of our hearts and transform them into new creations [in His likeness] fruit-bearing trees fit for paradise! The Bible is the tool He will use for the restoration or transformation of our hearts. No amount of working the mind or body can make us fit for heaven. It is the work of Christ on our hearts that will make us new. St. Paul writes, "Now this I say, brethren, that flesh and blood cannot inherit the Kingdom of God..." (1 Corinthians 15:50).

Physical death may come any moment; it may be quick and not as prolonged as it was for those on the Cross. Crucifixion is a slow death. Not everyone will have the opportunity to talk to Jesus in their last moments. We must do what we can do today: fear God and repent so we may enjoy God's presence and the tending or the working of His hands on our hearts. Even after 2000 and plus years, the world still debates if Jesus is truly the Son of God. Sceptics search for physical evidence of the garden when it is the transformed human hearts they need to see.

## Paradise

The apostle John was taken up in Spirit and shown a new heaven and a new earth. God is there. He writes, "...there shall in no wise enter into it anything that defileth..." (Revelation 21:27).

His description of paradise in the book of Revelation creates awe and wonder, for it is much more beautiful than the garden. What the garden was in the first creation, paradise is, in the new. The Tree of life and a river of the water of life is here. (Revelation 22:1,2)The garden belonged to the first Adam; paradise belongs to the last Adam - Jesus Christ, and those He has transformed or made new in His likeness. This world is like a quarry where all the chiselling, cutting and preparation of stone must be done, and transformation complete, ready to build the City of God. "And the house, when it was in building, was built of stone made ready before it was brought thither: so that there was neither hammer nor axe nor any tool of iron heard in the house, while it was in the building" (1 Kings 6:7).

The natural man or first Adam and all in his likeness will return to dust. Christ gives us spiritual life, the everlasting life! The spiritual or the second excels the natural! The last Adam or Jesus who came from heaven has returned to heaven. Jesus wants no one going their way but for all to go with Him to the place where He is gone. This is His promise to His disciples: "If I go and prepare a place for you, I will come again, and receive you unto myself; that where I am, there ye may be also" (John 14:3).

❀ ❀ ❀

# Bibliography

Bevan, Emma. F Arr. "None but Christ can satisfy". Sacred Songs and Solos. Sankey, Ira D. (compiled) Morgan & Scott Ltd., London. 1877. No:853. Print.

Hymnary.org. n.d. Praise Him, Praise Him.
[online] Available at: <https://hymnary.org/text/praise_him_praise_him_praise_him_in_the#instances> [Accessed 28 July 2021].

Lewis, C. S. *Mere Christianity*: *A Revised and Amplified Edition*. New York: HarperCollins Publishers, 2001.122. Print

Tozer. A. W. *The Dangers of a Shallow Faith*. Compiled and Edited by James L. Snyder. California: Regal, 2012. 20. Print (Tozer 1989)

Tozer. A. W. *Of God and Men*. Maharashtra, India: Alliance Publications, 1989. 61. Print

Tozer. A.W. *The Root of the Righteous*. Maharashtra, India: Alliance Publications, 1989. 7. Print

# Acknowledgement

My utmost gratitude and thanks to the LORD Almighty for drawing me to His presence and tending my heart with His Word.

With deep gratitude I acknowledge my dear parents, 'ma Sulochana and 'pa late Manson for all that they have been to me and for the Christian home they provided for me to grow in. Thanks 'ma for the encouragement and strength you continue to give to me and for being a model of living faith until this day.

My heartfelt gratitude to my dear husband Ranjit without whose support this book would not have come to be. Thanks to my beloved daughter Cynthia for designing the simple yet elegant book cover.

My sincere appreciation and thanks to my dear sister Thelma for the cover image and for editing the manuscript.

I acknowledge the many Churches that have contributed to my spiritual growth. I am also thankful for the many Christian authors whose books have helped shape my understanding of God and His purpose for humanity.

Thanks to Amazon's Kindle Direct Publishing for making it possible to have this book published.

# About The Author

## Linda Sigamony

Linda was born to Christian parents in Chennai, India. She immigrated to the United States of America, after she heard the LORD say to her, "Go to the land I will show you..." and while in this land, she found the treasure: Christ. She has experienced a spiritual birth and the words of the hymn, " None but Christ can satisfy" resonate with her soul.

O Christ, in Thee, my soul hath found,
And found in Thee alone
The peace, the joy I sought so long,
The bliss till now unknown

Now none but Christ can satisfy,
None other name for me
There's love, and life, and lasting joy,
Christ Jesus found in Thee.

(Attributed to Bevan, Emma F. 1877)

Linda is a physician turned theologian (self-made), called to write. She has written articles for the Annual Literary Journal: Reflections published by The Artist Circle of The Moody Church in Chicago, from 2014-2018 and for souvenirs released by the Church of South India Family and Youth Conference of North America 2017 and 2019, and a couple of articles for CSI Christ Church of Chicago.
She writes what grows from the Word of God within her soul. "He that abideth in me, and I in him, the same bringeth forth much fruit" (John 15:5) is a verse that has stayed in her heart from her

childhood. Her faith is rooted in Christ the LORD and has come to bear fruit.

She has a passion for Christ and The Church. She has been a Sunday School teacher for more than a decade, and is a voracious reader of Christian literature and The Bible. She loves to play hymns on the piano and sing. She lives in Chicago with her husband and daughter who is pursuing her University education.

Author contact: Lindasigamony@gmail.com

## Books By This Author

### Loaves Of Bread

A Collection of Contemplative Writings for Spiritual Growth

www.ingramcontent.com/pod-product-compliance
Lightning Source LLC
LaVergne TN
LVHW041236080426
835508LV00011B/1239